Rocks in the Path

By
Paul Holland

Copyright © 2010 by Paul Holland
All rights reserved.
No part of this book may be used or reproduced in any manner whatsoever without the written permission of the publisher.
Published by The SWG Group LLC, Little Falls, NJ
PAPERBACK ISBN 978-0-9722059-9-3

I would like to dedicate this book to my mother, who always found time to read to us...

Forward:

Who am I to write this? People will wonder why and frankly I am a little surprised myself. I am not some great biblical scholar or theologian. I am not a priest or minister. But I have spent over half a century asking and pondering many of these questions. Now that I'm on "the downhill side" let's say that I felt compelled to record some of what I have found along the way. It is my attempt to reconcile the secular mind to God.

Although it is generally based on Christian beliefs it is meant to be non-sectarian. There are those may take some of my words as an assault on their religion. This work isn't intended to challenge any institution, quite the contrary. Organized religion plays an integral role in bringing us closer to God but it is still a creation of man. Faith emanates from God. Sadly there will always be those who would twist belief to serve their personal ambitions. Unfortunately such behavior gives an excuse to those unfulfilled souls who decry religion, leaving little or nothing of value to replace it.

Great good has been done in the name of religion. So has great evil but that good and that evil was man's doing, not God's.

There sometimes comes a point in our lives where the road forks and people feel that they must either accept dogma without question or reject religion. There is a third path I believe; where people sort through the baggage we've accumulated in our lives and having discarded those weighty notions of little value, we shoulder our bundles and struggle on the path toward truth. It is the process by which we become the person we hope to present to God at the end of days. I will fail or succeed in my own way on my own path and trust to His mercy and charity. I share part of my climb to reach this place with you now in the hopes it will help you with your journey.

There are those who will applaud these words. There are those who will analyze and agonize over them. Others will dismiss this as the ravings of a lunatic or the scheme of a charlatan. Some will condemn my path just as there are those who will denounce yours but I would rather fail having served my conscience than turn aside from my duty to my Maker as He has given me the ability to understand it.

Your fellow pilgrim,
Paul

By way of introduction, a parable.

Two men served a common master. He led them to the edge of a desert and gave each one half a bottle of water saying, "Here is more than you will need to cross. Travel to my house on the other side. I will be waiting for you there."

The first was a shrewd and worldly man who thought, this bottle is already half empty and this is all I have to cross this wasteland. So he set out, bartering and bargaining with others he met along the way. Through his clever dealings by the time he arrived at his destination he had managed to fill his bottle to the brim.

The master of the house stopped him and said, "You don't need all this water you have collected and carried. All that you will ever need and more is waiting for you inside but you will need to leave your old bottle behind."

The man thought, this is just some trick to get my water. I labored for this, I suffered for it. I can't simply give it up now and so he turned his back and tightly clutching his bottle wandered once more back out into the burning sands.

The second man received the exact same measure of water but saw it differently because his master's instruction lingered with him, "Here is more than you will need to cross." He looked upon the bottle and thought, this is half full.

He used what he needed, sparingly and when he encountered others in need wandering along the way he would share what he carried. After all his master had assured him he had more than enough. If they were lost, he would point them in the direction of his master's house.

His journey was as hard and long as the first man's. By the time he arrived at the door his bottle was as empty and dry as the wasteland he had crossed. His master welcomed him in, saying, "You have brought me the perfect gift, an empty vessel waiting to be filled."

Welcome.

What is wisdom?

Wisdom is the object lesson that hides in our experiences. It is the part most worth keeping. Although people tend not to attach any direct value to it, wisdom's job is to help us make better choices (usually by avoiding the same mistakes).

Unfortunately, wisdom often seems to develop a little trouble with traction - it doesn't always "stick".

Its acquisition is often preceded by such phrases as "What was I thinking…" followed closely by the realization that we were not. In the absence of the second part, don't worry – the lesson will almost certainly be repeated. Repetition is the handmaiden of habit after all. The question is, which will you acquire first - wisdom or the bad habit? That is the heart of the dilemma.

Used long enough wisdom becomes a good habit and fits itself to us just like a comfortable old pair of shoes, until we hardly notice it. However like that old pair of shoes we can choose to leave it behind in the bottom of our closet. Electing to wear something new, shiny and stylish that pinches our toes instead. Of course we cannot walk or run nearly as far or as fast. We slip and trip and our feet will hurt at the end of the day but the rest of the crowd dressed in their shiny, new shoes will smile approvingly.

So I will ask you – is wisdom knowing the truth? Or is it remaining prudently silent?

In literature (and in life) wisdom is often relegated to be the purview of fools. That is why I am here.

I'll be your fool for the evening.

What is the greatest gift we have?

Have you ever agonized over a gift for someone only to have them open it and look disappointed or worse, indifferent? At least disappointment is an emotional response.

Have you ever known someone who can always manage to find fault, something to complain about?

We live in an imperfect world, inhabited by imperfect beings. If your objective is to find things to object to – you never have to search very hard. You'll find it but why would you want to waste your precious time looking? Aren't there better things to see? Yet we all fall victim at times. We are all guilty of focusing on the darker side of life. The problem is when it becomes habit and robs us of the ability to see anything else. People who do this always see themselves as the "victims". Sadly, their lives become a self-fulfilling prophesy because they surrender control over their daily existence to circumstance and other people.

There is an old saying that misery loves company. It seems as though the world around us conspires to steal our joy but it cannot do it without our willing consent. We have the ability to choose, to reject misery and replace it with something positive. The great news is that the good things in our lives are easy to find too, you need only stop and count your blessings for a moment to realize that.

An old friend of mine, Rollin Lee used to say that happiness is not a destination. It is a means of travel. It is a pity it took me so many years to learn just how wise he was. My advice is to buy a ticket and get on board early.

The greatest gift we can give ourselves, our friends, our families, our co-workers or to God - is a thankful heart. That is a habit worth cultivating.

The thankful heart doesn't have to stop to count its blessings because it never stops counting in the first place. When it encounters hardship, it rolls up its sleeves and says thank you for sleeves. Do you know someone like that? Then say thank you for sending this person to me as an example of what I could be too.

The crazy part is that when we see someone with a truly thankful heart we are often jealous, we covet it – but it is ours for the asking. We need only open our eyes and our ears and our minds to the wonderful things that lie all around us, that reside within us, and be glad. Don't worry, because a thankful heart never runs dry. The more you use it the more you will find within it.

The best part of a thankful heart is that it blesses everyone it touches. People will seek you out. They will want to be near you. Some because they want to learn from you, share with you and recharge their own positive energy. There will be those still living in darkness. They will come drawn like moths to a flame. Some are hoping to bask in the light, others are hoping to see you falter and fail. Make the gift available to all because misery may love company but company loves a thankful heart.

A thankful heart opens the door for all good graces.

This is the 21st century – times have changed, haven't they?

That is certainly true, from the standpoint of technology.

We have the ability to travel farther and faster than ever before – but where are we going in such a hurry?

We can see and talk to people half a world away in nanoseconds – but are we any better at listening to them?

We can accumulate veritable mountains of information, sort it, send it – but has it made us any wiser?

We can split the atom – but will we use that power to light cities or level them?

Yes, there is much that has changed over the millennia but human nature has not. We still fear, hope, envy, dream, love and hate…All our faults and failings are in full vigor, only our tools are more powerful.

So while times may have changed, we as beings have not.

Some things are eternal.

Why do we even need God?

Secular man attempts to bend nature and the universe to his will. He is consumed by a need to know, to be in control, to dominate. He must be master of all he surveys, answerable to none, supremely confident in his own abilities. What makes him truly dangerous is that he cannot be honest with himself regarding his own limitations. He is governed by his own base nature, his own unrelenting appetites held in check by his moral compass... or not. Left to his own devices, he will push as far, as fast as he can – until something pushes back. God is the last thing he wants. Look around at the world those ideals have created.

Dwindling natural resources, Pollution, Famine, Violence, War, Intolerance, Indifference, Gross over consumption...

In the 1800 years following the birth of Christ, the human population increased by less than 5 fold. In the next 100 years by 1900, it had increased 8 fold. Today a century after that, the number has swollen to more than 30 fold.

This is meant neither as an indictment nor as an endorsement of population control.

I cite these facts as an example because every one of the over six billion beings that now inhabit our planet is driven by those same human frailties that formed and governed our behavior 2000 years ago but there are two critical factors that have changed.

The moral compass that held society in check for centuries was a function of the traditional nuclear family and the church. Today both of these mainstays have been eroded and subsequently this critical foundation of social structure is often being replaced by government, legislation and popular culture.

The second critical factor that has been increasing is an almost blind reliance on technology to solve our problems. Ironic since many of our present difficulties are in fact the direct or indirect result of "technological advances". The explosion in population cited earlier is only one example. Technology pulled the cork from the bottle. We grow more food but it didn't eliminate hunger – because our technology has also managed to create more hungry people. It is estimated that enough food is grown currently to feed twice the earth's existing population, yet in many places millions starve every year and many millions more suffer from malnutrition while obesity has become a leading contributor to millions of deaths elsewhere. It is insanity. It is obscene.

There are two primary reasons. First, technology is a function of knowledge and all knowledge is limited. We often don't see the potential ripple effects of what we do. Second, the secular man cares about the outcome he wants right now and blithely turns a blind eye to the rest.

The secular person exists in the vacuum of an egocentric universe. The future is an abstract. The natural world is a thing to be used, conquered, and exploited. Other people are viewed as competition, as underlings, as statistics, in some cases as prey. In that, he is no different than any other animal, existing by the law of the jungle. It is said that power corrupts and absolute power corrupts absolutely. When man thinks he is the ultimate power on earth what horrors can he unleash and without any sense of something greater to stop him, how can we hope to survive? We already know... we have seen the previews... Hitler, Stalin, the trail of tears, the rape of Nanking... the list is as old and bloody as mankind's history.

Once we have adopted a belief in God, in acknowledging His existence we must also admit that God is not "us". We are answerable to a greater power.

Further, when we accept that a divine spark resides in us, we must also logically admit that it can be found in our fellow beings - we are no longer isolated. We are part of a greater family. Both individually and collectively we hold each other to a higher standard. Our moral and ethical treatment of one other and our stewardship of the earth take on a new imperative that simply does not exist in the secular view.

This is not to say that man has not perverted and twisted religious conviction to serve worldly ends, he has. However those are cases where the secular mind was at work, using others to achieve some personal agenda. Such actions and their actors do not disprove the need for God. In fact they show all the more the need to keep Him in the picture.

God is good for us.

People talk about "God's plan"... What is God's plan?

God's plan is God's plan. I don't know what it is. How could anyone know what it is? I could no more take it in than I could swallow the ocean.

There are those who believe that each individual destiny is mapped out but if we are agents of free will how could that be? We are not bugs trapped in amber or chess pieces on the board of the universe to be moved about by some unseen hand.

Instead of worrying about what God is doing, the better question is - What am I doing? How do I play my part in all this? A foot soldier doesn't need to know the global battle strategy. He simply needs to know what he has to do. At best, we are afforded some glimpses of what purposes may be in store for us.

We delude ourselves when we try to fit our idea of what God's plan "should be" to the universe. For example, intelligent design is an attempt to fit a spiritual answer to a secular question. Why? Science cannot disprove the existence of God any more than religion can negate the findings of science. Whenever new facts are unearthed that demonstrate the infinite complexities of the universe, I marvel at the fact that we are a part of all this. Isn't that enough? I don't know exactly when or how creation occurred and frankly, it really doesn't make any difference to me. It doesn't matter how many angels can dance on the head of a pin either.

What matters is where we go from here, today, right now. That being said –

What is your plan?

A question of infinity...

The secular mind loves questions like, "What did God do before creation?" or "If the universe is infinite, it wouldn't have a beginning or end – so how could God have created it?"

It is amazing to me that people will use a term like "infinite" as if we could actually grasp its meaning. I recall seeing one calculation regarding the mass of the observable universe. It was estimated to be 3×10^{52} Kilograms. This is a number so enormous that its scale defies human comprehension.

Here are the flies in that ointment...

Take 3×10^{52} and multiply it times itself, ten million times. Now do it again and again, you still have not scratched the surface of infinity. It may be a huge number but it is still a finite number. The human mind defines things by their limits because we have limits. Limits are what we understand.

Infinity has no limits and by definition cannot have any. For that reason, we do not and cannot understand it. We have no frame of reference for such a concept. Take it a step further...

The statement says this value describes the mass of the _observable_ universe. Our eyes cannot see things like radio waves or subatomic particles but we can detect them so we know they exist. We cannot hear ultra high frequency sounds, but we can detect them so we know they exist.

We know what we know – but we have no idea how much we don't know.

Our minds must struggle to grasp finite principles. Why are we so anxious about trying to box in the infinite? I believe it is because it frightens us that something so vast could exist beyond our ability to even take it in. Despite all our efforts to place Him there, God does not fit neatly on a shelf.

All statements of fact, the laws of nature and science come with a disclaimer that goes like this, "There is no intelligent life on Mars, _as we know it_." That is how the secular mind covers its "belief" system.

In church, we just say…

"God, who passes all understanding…"

So is technology bad?

The root of the word "technology" comes from Greek and basically means "the knowledge of tools and their use".

Technology is merely a tool, like fire or a hammer. Such things are neither good nor bad, they simply are. I can use fire to light and heat a house or burn it to the ground. I can use a hammer to rebuild that house or to strike and kill its inhabitants. Tools have no direction other than that which we give them.

All too often, regardless of how noble the motives of a technology's creator, the deciding factor of it's employment is not the betterment of mankind but rather the lining of someone's pockets...The more powerful the technology the greater the responsibility and alas, the temptation to abuse it.

Technology is not self-directing. It lacks the ability to challenge the wisdom and motives of the person wielding it. That is up to us.

Tools have an excuse – they lack souls.

Is Jesus Christ the son of God?

The acceptance of His divinity is the cornerstone of Christian belief which cites scripture, most notably John 3:16 – "For God so loved the world, as to give His only begotten Son; that whosoever believeth in Him, may not perish, but may have life everlasting."

But beliefs vary. Some people reject his divinity outright. Others may call Him a prophet. There are those who believe Jesus was only a man but still might acknowledge His capacity as a teacher and sage.

Whether you believe in His divinity is a question for each individual heart to answer – but even if you can not or do not, <u>can you accept the validity of what Jesus espoused</u>?

In his book <u>Christianity and the Crisis in Cultures</u> written by Cardinal Joseph Ratzinger prior to becoming Pope Benedict XVI, he points out that the social necessity for a moral compass would exist "etsi Deus non daretur," even if God did not. That is quite a position for a man in his position, to even suggest such a leap.

When one considers values such as compassion, tolerance, forgiveness, and charity, it makes you wonder how much better and kinder a world this might be if we made an effort to live by those simple precepts?

We are all God's children and like all relatives we can and will have our disagreements, but in that same spirit of family shouldn't we all try to seek these higher things? No one has or should have a monopoly on respect and dignity. Traditions and customs vary, truth does not. It is not selective. Although the appearance of truth can be twisted and warped by man to serve his ends, in the final balance what is true and just either applies to all or none. Like the words of Jesus, the answer is simple. Putting it into practice is the hard part.

We should love one another.

How could we be created in God's image, we're all so different?

That is true. These corporeal shells we wear come in all different sizes, shapes and colors.

Being created in His image must then have a different and deeper meaning. One based not on appearance but rather on some essence that we all hold in common. It must be some aspect that draws and binds people together in our quest to be more like our creator.

Certainly, logically, it follows that it could not be something that splits us apart... right?

What if we assume that we were all created with the capacity to love, by love? We were created with the capacity to be faithful, by faith. We were created with the capacity to hope, in the eternal hope that we make our way back to Him.

Might that be our soul, our divine spark...?

What about stories like Adam and Eve?

For the purpose of this discussion, let us agree that the purpose of scripture is to help us understand and build a better relationship with God.

What if we look beyond the language of Genesis and see it just as a story, a parable if you will? What if Adam and Eve were named Fred and Sally? What if they ate a fig instead of an apple? Would the story change in any substantial way? No, not really.

It is a story about how as beings we have permitted our own failings, our weakness to temptation, our inability to get out of our own way to distance us from God, from paradise. It is a story about how even when we had everything our hearts could desire, we rejected it all because some flaw in our nature compelled us to reach for the one and only thing that was forbidden and we fell. It is a story about how the knowledge of our folly leaves us feeling naked, vulnerable and ashamed. Is that a story you can get behind?

Don't throw the baby (or the bible) out with the bathwater.

Is there a Heaven or Hell?

Scripture tells us they exist but I would put the following to you...

When I was a child and my father asked me to do something, I would do it. I knew if I complied he would be happy with me. I might even be rewarded in some fashion, if only a pat on the back. I also knew if I didn't do as I was asked I'd get in trouble, perhaps be punished in some way. But I was a child then...

Today I am a grown man with grown children of my own. I am far beyond my father's ability to reward or punish, yet if he asked me to do something – I would do it. I would do it because I love him...because I respect and honor him. I would do it simply because it is the right thing to do.

As a mature person, why should I need any other inducement?

Belief in the resurrection is the lynchpin of Christianity. For that reason I understand what I am about to say may shake some people up...

Is that all there is to religion, the promise of the carrot and threat of the stick? The shame is that many people get stuck at that point in the development of their faith. After all, if you are certain of your place in Heaven, change is the last thing you want. Why would you question it?

Unfortunately, it leaves those who crave God but struggle with accepting church teachings on the outside looking in. Alone, their feelings all too often turn to anger, sarcasm and apathy. But ask yourself - If you serve God only to win a place in Heaven and/or avoid eternal punishment, are you truly serving Him – or your own self interests? Shouldn't we love and serve God, simply because He is God?

The real question should be; if there were no promise of heaven or threat of hell – would you still seek to do God's will?

Assume heaven and hell do exist, what would they be like?

Both sacred and secular works have attempted to depict them for centuries. Newer media such as movies have a field day with their interpretations.

Personally, I believe that the existence of heaven and hell and the form that they might assume are exactly whatever God wishes them to be. No more, no less and I don't worry about it.

I also believe the defining characteristic of heaven is God's presence. Just as the defining characteristic of hell would be His absence.

If we see God as the infinite source of that which is good, loving and just; what greater reward could there be than to be joined with Him eternally?

What greater punishment might there be than to be severed from Him?

Assume there is a heaven, how do I get there?

Although different sects impose their own views, universally Christian dogma and the bible tell us basically two things are required.

The first is to accept the gift of salvation purchased by the crucifixion of Jesus.

The second is to live a life worthy of that gift to the best of our ability.

In my experience it is easier to accept the sacrifice of another than to live a life worthy of it.

Naturally, non-Christian denominations have their own belief systems, but I think we do best when we forget about trying to save ourselves. Instead, simply live a life that is such an example of what we can all be that it inspires others around us to seek God, and in the process help them to find a saving grace in their own lives.

Be the grace you would receive.

If God is perfect, why doesn't He just fix everything?

Worldwide, there are approximately 45 million people who are blind. Estimates of people who are hearing impaired globally range from about 22 to 36 million. There are 135,000 amputees in America alone each year. In the time it takes to read this paragraph, five more people will have starved to death. It is endless.

If God is omnipotent and He loves us, why doesn't He just fix it? Why leave us trapped in a world of violence, weakness, disease and corruption?

Great question, but it is the wrong question. Why do we choose this corrupt violent, diseased world instead of God? He shows us the way and we reject it — so who is crazy, God or us?

Our stay here is insignificant in the annals of history but our impact on how we respect or hurt one another and the world that surrounds us can echo through time.

I suppose that God could react perfectly to every situation, but maybe that's not the point.

Maybe it is about how we react.

What about Satan?

If you believe in God as the source of all that is good, it stands to reason that His counterpart must also exist. Otherwise there is no balance. Good would simply reign and evil would be extinguished. Just as God seeks to work His will by enlisting us, it makes sense that evil would try to work through us as well.

This one may boggle your mind.

As imperfect beings, possessing the capacity for both good and evil we are trapped in that balance. It is our free will, our ability to choose how we behave toward each other and our world at large that tip the scales.

Satan must exist just as Judas had to, in order for God's will to be accomplished. After all without an alternative that we can choose – free will cannot exist, it would be meaningless and our ability to grow would be impossible.

If God were the only choice, there would be no choice. Free will requires that we must both elect one and reject the other.

Each day, with each breath, we choose.

So do evil and hardship serve some divine purpose...

A very short parable: A man left a chain on a shelf because he didn't know if it was strong enough for the job.

Both man and chain are unfulfilled. We never know the strength of a chain or a man until they reach their breaking point

To get better at anything, we need to strain our limits. Hardship is not evil, it is just difficult. Dealing with hardship makes us physically and emotionally tougher. Battling evil makes us stronger spiritually.

The right path often leads uphill. Temptation usually doesn't come with warning labels, wrapped in barbed wire. As a rule, sin is usually very attractive and it is so tempting to throw up our hands and surrender to despair at times.

Perhaps that is why people refer to it as "exercising" free will. It is the strength and pull of evil that makes the victory of truth and justice all the greater but it also makes our journey through life perilous.

Only great challenges yield great victories.

If the Bible is God's Word, why are there so many inconsistencies?

The bible contains God's Word, but not necessarily His words.

The bible is written in the words of men and we are imperfect beings. Language is at its best a very flawed means of communication. For example; <u>Lead</u> is a heavy metal or I can <u>lead</u> you out of the wilderness. I can pour myself a <u>drink</u> or I can <u>drink</u> something. Words alone often have different meanings and alternative uses. The definition of words changes dramatically over time. To be gay used to mean you were happy and smoking pot referred to something forgotten on the stove. A simple change in punctuation can radically alter a sentence or phrase. Consider the following:

> I love God more than you.

What does it mean? Does it mean "I love God more than I love you", or does it mean "I love God more than you love God"? Language is filled with pitfalls.

Some proponents will assert that the bible must be taken word for word – literally, exactly as written. Isn't it ironic that detractors and skeptics insist on exactly the same thing? Both groups quote passages from the same work in order to prove or disprove diametrically opposed positions. It's because they occupy the same space at opposite extremes. Both insist it must be all right or it must be all wrong. How many things in the realm of human existence are all right or all wrong?

People can argue over the words of men, but not the Word of God, that is to say the spirit, the meaning and mystery that underlies the work.

We need to look beyond the words to the message they convey. In Genesis would it change the fabric of the story if Methuselah lived 970 years instead of 969? Would it matter if the Ark were 301 cubits long instead of 300? Debating such facts is like arguing over specks in the pepper?

When Christ's adversaries sought to trick Him into committing heresy, they went to Jesus and asked, "Which one of God's commandments is the greatest?"

He shocked them by not quoting from scripture. He said to simply love God and love your neighbor. He knew that if we obey those most basic precepts we can not help but keep the rest. That was the spirit of the commandments revealed, the unwritten words, the Word of God.

Have you ever heard anyone refute that? Are there any inconsistencies there? If so I cannot find them.

The words of men are corruptible and easily misunderstood. Sadly, as poor a means of communication as language is, it is still all we have. In the absence of any other medium, the bible seeks to communicate the infinite using finite terms, perfection using a flawed and broken system that creaks and groans under the strain.

The Word of God begins where the words of men fail.

If you want to truly understand a book written in another tongue, it is not enough to speak it, you must be able to think in that language. The bible is an attempt on the part of people, motivated by the Holy Spirit, to capture something divine in human terms.

Scripture can be read in the language of men but it cannot truly be understood until we find the same Spirit that moved the authors within ourselves to translate it into our hearts. Without that, they will forever remain only words on a page.

The Word of God is not inconsistent; we are in our inability to translate it.

How about the 10 Commandments and all the other laws in the bible?

At the dawn of Genesis, there was only one commandment, "Don't eat of this tree." It couldn't have been simpler. Original sin was not the literal or symbolic eating of an apple – it was turning away from God.

As human society and all its attendant problems grew, the 10 commandments were given, and then came the codification of laws. As we moved farther from God, law gradually replaced our moral compass but it was always incomplete. Laws only beget more laws.

Today, we commonly ask whether or not something is legal instead of whether or not it is the right thing to do. Laws have loopholes. Morality, truth and justice do not.

In the establishment of His new covenant, Jesus overturns the body of law. In fact, He defied the law when on the Sabbath He healed the sick. To perform any work on the Lord's Day was forbidden. His disciples broke that law by picking grain on the Sabbath because they were hungry. He stopped the crowd from stoning the woman but the people were legally justified. Scripture said they were supposed to execute her.

Christ shatters the law when He puts forward His two "new" commandments. But then, men are bound by laws, not God. It was a call to find within ourselves that sense of a moral being again. He was showing us how to shorten the distance between God and man. That answer is not found in any courtroom or books of law, it is found in us, or not at all.

Our own heart should be our harshest judge and sharpest critic.

Why do bad things happen to good people – Or - why do people profit by evil ways?

If God is omnipotent and just, why does He permit injustice to occur?

The short answer is that God does not permit injustice – we do. God simply permits us to choose our own paths – for a purpose.

No one ever asks why do good things happen to good people or why do bad things happen to bad people?

Consider for a moment, that if only "bad things" happened to "bad people" - how would we ever have the opportunity to practice forgiveness, patience, tolerance, mercy, charity... We wouldn't. People would simply "get what they deserved." Think about your own faults and ask, is that really what you want?

The simple reality of this world is that things happen to people. For all of us, good and bad, rich and poor – life and death do not discriminate. The sum total of who we are physically, emotionally, intellectually and spiritually is a constantly evolving process. When things happen, as they will and must, a battle between all that we are guides our next step. That step in turn becomes part of the total of our being. Each decision we make in time helps to guide us as we move forward... all the more reason to place our feet carefully because we will carry the indelible mark of all those decisions with us. As in any wilderness, once we have strayed from the path it becomes increasingly difficult to find our way again. It's all part of the process of becoming. We are all works in progress. Even God does not presume to judge us until the end of days.

The better questions are; when bad things happened to good people, where were we and what did we do?

What made Christ angry?

Whenever I have asked that question, I generally get a puzzled look.

He made a whip to drive the money changers from the temple. An act of violence from the Prince of Peace – it doesn't seem to make sense. Consider how He chastised Peter on the eve of His crucifixion. How He admonished the crowd poised to stone the woman. What angered Christ was hypocrisy. Let he who is without sin cast the first stone. Seek not to remove the mote from your brother's eye until you have removed the log from your own. Judge not lest ye be judged.

Hypocrisy is the most insidious of sins because it emanates from a sense of self-righteousness that allows us to excuse our actions no matter how heinous.

Hypocrisy is a lie we tell ourselves.

Herein lays the great danger. It is an inherent flaw of man that just as soon as we believe we are right, by definition everyone else must be wrong. As soon as we begin to believe we can judge others we place ourselves above them.

Jesus humbled himself before the meanest and most base of his enemies to be judged by them. Even though He knew the result of that judgment would not be based on justice, wisdom or mercy – but instead on anger, fear and greed. These faults are part of us, the legacy of man and knowing that I would ask;

Who among us is truly fit to judge his fellow creatures?

Who will be saved?

Religion struggles with questions such as; what would happen to a man who never heard of Christ yet lived a wholly Christian life? The strict dogma of some churches point to biblical passages, notably John 14:6, "... I am the way, the truth, and the life: no man cometh unto the Father, but by Me." stating that a strict interpretation requires an affirmed belief in Jesus for salvation.

Religion feels compelled to try to answer such questions, but what if that passage means something else? What if it simply means that God and not us will make that call. Didn't Jesus shun the pious to dine with harlots and sinners? Faith says; trust God to work it out.

Religion is an imperfect creation of man and as odd as it sounds, it segregates us. It builds walls which by definition must both include and exclude people. Each has its own rules of order and rituals.

Faith emanates from God as a force to make us whole, it seeks to build bridges between each other and our Creator. Rather than committing the words of scripture to memory – why not commit yourself to the spirit of scripture? Words can be misquoted, twisted, taken out of context. The spirit that underlies the words is incorruptible. It transcends mere language, culture and creed that can drive wedges between us. When we focus on that which sets us apart, that is all we see. Why not look for what we have in common instead?

I was once asked whether I thought it was possible for a man to earn his way to heaven through his actions. I replied I don't know if a man could win a place in heaven by what he does. It is up to God to read a man's heart... but I do believe by our actions and inactions we can certainly distance ourselves from God. What greater hypocrisy is there than to profess your faith and then not live it?

I am mortal and what eternity may hold is beyond my poor comprehension. It is enough for me to do right with those gifts that God has seen fit to entrust me with, at least in my own faulty way.

When I close my eyes in that last long sleep that is death I will be content to trust myself to His mercy. We can do no more and should endeavor to do no less.

When religion runs out of answers, try faith.

What if you are born again?

People will tell you that they are born again. That is not enough. We must live again.

We do not aspire to heaven in a single leap. We earn our way – or lose it with each step we take.

If you could be born again in this world with the next breathe you draw you are still human and subject to all our frailties. Christ got tired, He got hungry, He got angry, He was tempted. What hope do we have? It is not enough to be born again unless you can shake off the shackles of human weakness.

To be born again means that you must recognize you are an infant beginning a life-long journey. You must be willing to grow in that new direction.

The danger in fundamentalist thought is that secure in the knowledge of a seat in heaven it is so easy fall into the snares of hypocrisy and pride. Christ prayed for guidance. How is it that any of us can presume to have all the answers? Christ did not pray to change those who were different from Himself, even those who hated Him. He asked only for the strength to forgive and show those people the mercy and tolerance they were unwilling or unable to give to Him. How then can we condemn, how can we be so self-righteous, how can we be intolerant of the paths of others and still say that we have truly accepted Him into our hearts?

I cannot be born again in this world through any act or word of mine, but I can in my limited capacity try to follow that glimmer of truth and meaning that lie beyond the written page. It is toward that light that I must continue to struggle and trust in that greater mercy that is God. When and if I am born again it will be because He says so, not because I do.

It is not enough to be born again, until you are ready to live anew.

What is sin?

I believe that sin derives from selfishness, having a greater concern for oneself than for God or those around us.

There is a good reason that the Ten Commandments include coveting. We live a world that has succumbed to the "myth of more than enough". We need only enough, our daily bread but we all desire more than enough, don't we? The shame is that it can never be fulfilled. There is always something more to catch our eye. It not only empties our pockets – it leaves us spiritually and emotionally bankrupt as well, forever wanting and dissatisfied.

The fastest road to unhappiness I know is counting the fortunes of others. I try not to envy or dread the paths others must walk. That is between themselves and God, the goal where it is hoped ultimately all ways will lead.

The material world turns our attention inward and keeps us focused there but it comes with a terrible price.

Consumerism ultimately consumes us.

It prohibits us from seeing beyond ourselves, it retards our growth spiritually. It winds itself through our daily lives and distorts our priorities.

Try this simple exercise; first – make a list of what you think is truly important in your life. Then keep a log of your time for one week. You will spend time on what you truly value. Be warned, you may not like what you see.

Like the man who buried his talent in the ground, sin hides the potential entrusted to us by our Master where it will do little or no good for anyone. Whatever the reason; greed, fear, envy, laziness, even just habit – when we choose the path of "self" it limits our ability to grow in faith and it will also exact a toll from the lives around us. The result is inevitable.

Sin is putting self first.

What is the greatest sin?

According to dogma, the seven deadly sins are: avarice, wrath, gluttony, pride, lust, envy and sloth. All of these are sins of commission except one. We commit acts of anger, lust and vanity – greed, and excess, we actively covet.

Only sloth is a sin of omission. It is about not doing, not caring. It abandons us to listlessness, helplessness. It leaves us devoid of hope.

Sloth, accidie, apathy, call it what you will; it paves the path to other sins because it traps us within ourselves. We become the very chains that bind us to earth. Ironically, we must choose other sins but sloth requires only that we settle for less than our potential, that we surrender power and control. What do we get in return for this... mediocrity, despair, isolation? Not a very good trade.

God offers us hope and why wouldn't He? If we consider Him as the source of our potential, it only makes sense that He would give us the foundation stone from which to build successfully. He wants us to excel.

Hope grants us the power to reject the ignominy and decay of sloth and by that empowerment find the strength we need to become the best that we can be.

Our potential lies hidden, locked away in a dungeon of sin, self-doubt and denial that we construct around ourselves. Sloth guards that door but God has furnished us the key, the first step back to the fresh air and light.

Hope is a choice we make.

What if you repent?

We are told salvation is a gift. It is a gift because, despite our best efforts – we are and will always be imperfect. God's mercy, His gift must "make up the difference" when our souls are found wanting.

It is not our place or our nature to be perfect but it is our obligation to do the best we can with those talents and abilities that God has seen fit to entrust to us in spite of our shortcomings. Consider the parable of the widow's mite. (Mark 12:41-44 and Luke 21:1-4)

A truly repentant heart knows it honors God's gift of forgiveness best by working to reduce our need for it, at least to try our best in that regard.

When we profess our faith, we build a bridge to God.

When we live our faith, we pay the toll to cross that bridge.

What will you pay to cross?

Why does God grant us free will, and then ask us to do His Will?

It is even tougher than that.

The obvious answer is that God wants us to choose His way rather than another. Who wouldn't prefer the worship of willing supplicants over that of mindless slaves?

But there is much more...

It is not a question of surrendering your will or my will. That implies God wins and we lose but that isn't the case. It is not a competition, a battle of wills. If it were what chance would we stand? God chooses not to impose His Will.

It is only false pride in our own abilities that holds us back. It is hubris to think that we always know better. Why not take joy in sharing a greater vision? Why not rely upon a deeper wisdom?

It is about collaboration, not conquest.

Then why doesn't God just make His Will known?

With regard to "the big picture" there is of course the bible, the commandments...

On a personal level, God doesn't issue memos. He doesn't take billboard space or send out email. We must discern His Will. We have to work at it, for good reasons.

Doing His Will is more than simply following orders from the "Big Boss". Consider for a moment, is there anything you can do that God could not do better? Of course not... so it is not about doing "stuff".

What God truly wants and values is a relationship. Consider for a moment, isn't the definition of a consummate friendship one where you seem to know what each other is thinking without saying a word? You are that much in tune with one another. But every relationship requires that we work at it. It doesn't happen overnight – it requires effort.

If you want to get in shape physically, you gradually increase the amount of weights you lift and the number of repetitions you do. You gradually increase how far and fast you run AND you do it every day. You can't go to a gym twice a year and get stronger.

If you want better relationships with your family and friends – talk with them, listen to them, all the time, not just on your terms. Why should we think having a sound and loving relationship with God would require any less?

You have to want it enough to work at it.

Why did Christ insist that we give what we have to the poor?

Christ admonished us to give away all that we have but it wasn't to enrich the poor. After all, He also said, "The poor will be with you always."

The Christian concept of charity is not about the re-distribution of wealth. That is incidental. Wasn't the gift of the widow's mite more highly prized than the rich man's alms? God has no use for earthly riches.

The act of charity frees two people. It frees the person in want from gnawing hunger, cold, ignorance and isolation… the burden of simply existing moment to moment. It also frees the giver from the clutches of materialism that bind him to this place. Scripture says no man can serve two masters…

Once freed, both have the opportunity to turn their hearts and minds to higher things.

You can hold more, once you are empty…

My prayers go unanswered. Does God listen? Does He care?

It is so tempting to answer that question dismissively but I know that pain of doubt that lies behind it. In the course of our lives who hasn't wondered about these things?

I believe in the power of prayer but its first, best purpose is not to ask for "things", regardless of how noble they might seem. For example; we could pray for world peace but how could God provide that without stripping mankind of free will? What if instead we prayed people find the strength and wisdom within their own hearts to just follow God's commandments. Wouldn't world peace and much more be the natural outcome?

Often we lack the wisdom to appreciate what it is we are truly asking for. God is not a wishing well. The purpose of prayer is not just "to ask", it is to converse. Prayer opens your heart and mind. It is about examining and understanding our own motives.

If we ask and then fail to listen for the answers how will we ever learn anything?

We often fear the solitude of quiet prayer because it leaves us alone with the chaos of our minds.

Meditating on that we begin to see how little control we have in our lives. It's frightening but as we order our thoughts, as we quiet the uproar of our existence we often find the answers that we seek, that strength we need, the clarity that eludes us. Yes, He cares.

If it seems God isn't listening to you, could it be you aren't listening to Him.

What constitutes church?

Christ referred to building His church. What shape did it take? What ground did it stand upon?

His church was firmly rooted in the hearts and minds of the people who heard and accepted His message. Roofs define and contain things. Walls keep people in and keep people out.

God seeks to include us not exclude us. We do that on our own.

What cathedral raised by the hand of man can compare to the miracle of a single blade of grass? The grandest structure of stone, glass and steel must pale in significance. The next time we think ourselves mighty as we survey our cities – consider the humble termite. Based on scale, they are every bit as much or more prolific builders.

Do our edifices truly glorify God, or ourselves? He was born in a stable.

A building is a lifeless and temporal thing. It is only as full or empty as the hearts that reside within it.

Consider further that a building can be finished. No matter how grand, there comes a day when the last nail is driven, the last block is laid... we as people are never finished until we lay the culmination of our humble efforts before the greatest builder of all in the hopes that He will call it good.

Every heart should be a church and every voice a choir. Worship there... every day. Good news, it is a short commute.

Does that mean I shouldn't go to church?

No, that's not what it means. Whether or not you actively attend church is entirely up to you (we have free will) but...

The practice of religion gives us form, substance and a sense of community. It keeps us connected. It can help us both to find and remain on our pathway to faith. Those are all good things.

We are creatures governed by habit, both good and bad. Good habits serve us. In the case of bad habits, we serve them.

Regular worship promotes many things. For example; it can help to keep us mindful of both God and our neighbor (there are those two commandments again). It can act as a conduit for ways to serve our community through good works and other charitable activities. It provides a means for us to get outside ourselves but like anything else we do — what we can only take from it a measure of what we put in.

If worship is simply going through the motions, if the homily is an opportunity for a quick nap, why are you there?

Religion should not be a substitute for faith. All too often people permit the progression of their relationship with God to be arrested because "they are saved, they are His chosen". Too often we see the church as an "instant fix" rather than a life-long climb.

Faith doesn't end in church – it begins there.

What church does God belong to?

God doesn't belong to a religion.
People do.

The act of "belonging" implies some form of ownership or membership. My shoes belong to me because I bought them in a store. I paid a fee to belong to a gym so that I could work out. What is amazing is the attempt by people to put boundaries around God.

God is not under contract. You cannot compel Him to perform. We have all seen chain letters and prayers, repeat this twenty times and you will get what you want... That's ridiculous. God doesn't work for us and He doesn't owe us anything.

We live in an age when everyone is concerned with their "rights" – maybe we should be a little more concerned with our "wrongs". The wrongs we do to God, to each other and to ourselves. The wrongs we do to this planet we have stewardship of. How many of us go to church for an hour, then place God neatly back on a shelf thankful that our obligation is over for another week, safe and secure in the knowledge that He's on our side.

If you spent that meager amount of time at your job each week, with your family each week, or with your friends each week... how long do you suppose it would be before you were unemployed, homeless and friendless?

What if God gave you the same level of commitment you gave to Him? If we want God to be responsible to our needs, we need to be responsible to Him and to each other. Here is where it gets interesting. By keeping God in our lives, our lives get better. We feel more fulfilled. We treat each other better. We practice compassion, understanding and forgiveness. We also foster those qualities in those around us so that we are repaid in kind. Believing, loving and serving God doesn't make our lives harder, it makes our lives better, richer, fuller...

The church God belongs to is us.

There are some things my church teaches that I don't agree with?

The purpose of church is to help us grow closer to God. If the doctrine of the church you attend is at odds with an opinion that you hold, such that it is halting your spiritual growth, you need to ask yourself two questions.

First, why do you disagree? What is the source of your conflict? Be brutally honest with yourself. Is it that you find yourself bowing to peer pressure instead of following your conscience? Is your confusion the result of conflicting and compelling arguments of fact or law? In other words - is the source of your doubt secular in nature? Do you find yourself thinking things like - *"I don't go along with the church because of what others may think – or – The church says this is wrong, but it is still legal…?"*

We have all felt that way at times. It isn't necessarily a bad thing. Truth doesn't fear debate but you must put it in perspective. At one point in time slavery was legal and it was a common practice. It is even condoned in the bible – did that make it right?

It is hard sometimes to remember that this is not the spiritual journey of your friends, your family, co-workers or government officials... this is your path. Don't surrender such an important decision to others. Only you get to answer this one.

The second question you should ask is if your disagreement with church doctrine is spiritual in nature. By that I mean, your conflict is with an official practice or position of the church that you feel is in defiance of God's will. This is not to be confused with the interpretation of any person or persons within the church. They may be trying to subvert doctrine for their own reasons or beliefs. There was a time when "God fearing" people arrested, tortured and executed their neighbors suspected of witchcraft, all in the name of the church.

We can all get it wrong – that is part of the price of free will.

Churches must try to serve a multitude of pathways to God by providing us with a general direction.

But we each must serve our own conscience in order to serve God.

Why are there some people always trying to convert others?

On one level, religions grow by attracting converts. That is pretty straight forward.

On another level, scripture calls upon people to be witnesses to their faith, to spread the word. There are religious mandates to spend time doing missionary work that some people take very literally.

Whether or not I may agree personally with their views I respect the fact that they are willing to live their faith, sometimes at the cost of a night in jail or a punch in the nose BUT where does that zeal cross the line... When does the promotion of what you believe cease to be spreading the word and become an indictment of what others believe? If I perceive your efforts as an attack on my faith, wouldn't that make me defend my position even more vigorously?

There is a very normal side of our natures that wants others to join with us. Man is a social animal and in a very real sense, when others share our beliefs we feel validated. We must be right because others are doing it too. Consider the vice of smoking. Intellectually we know that it is incredibly harmful. There is absolutely no good reason to smoke. Yet young people pressure each other to start. It may be foolish but if "everybody is doing it" we feel it somehow vindicates our behavior.

Back to proselytizing one's religion...

If you chase a dog, he runs away. If you simply treat him with kindness, he'll find you. Take a lesson from an old dog and first – don't drive people away.

For many faith is like a billboard you pass or radio ad you hear on your way to work. You know it is there somewhere in the back of your mind. No one has to tell you about it but it gets ignored. In our crazy, jumbled, over-communicated and over-scheduled society it fades to the level of white noise until something happens to change that. Suddenly we find a need for whatever that billboard or ad was promoting and its message leapfrogs to the front of our brain. We start searching for it during our commute. The point is that no one will ever hear the message until it is time... their time. You cannot convert another person by any argument or action. They can only convert themselves.

Take it up a notch. If you proclaim that you are a Christian, and do not act as one, what does that say? For each bad act on your part you undo the work of 10,000 good acts. Why... because your detractors will point to that one stumble that supports their opinion and ignore the rest. It is just human nature.

You can speak with the eloquence of angels but your actions will proclaim the truth or lie behind your words.

Before anyone can hope to convert another, we need to convert ourselves. The example of how you lead your life is the first most powerful witness of your faith. First – show me what you believe. Then you can tell me all about it because what you say vanishes in the wind, what you do echoes eternally.

If you want to spread your faith, live it.

What about a belief in technology and science?

Science and technology have for many people become a de facto religion but I would pose the following:

Such a belief sets the human mind up as supremely powerful based on our ability to reason and learn. Yet what we know is infinitesimally small compared to what we don't know.

Simply because we can learn, doesn't mean we do... How often has man repeated the same mistakes again and again? We are fallible. Is that worthy of our faith?

We are capable of logic and reason, but torn by emotions which can cloud it and delude us.

Human knowledge and technology is not based on the creation of a thing, but only on the manipulation of what already exists. We are inherently limited.

At some point even the most rock solid science requires a leap of faith that the results of a given action will always prove consistent. That is why science hates words like always and never. Does it make sense to place our unquestioning faith in something where changing even a single parameter can radically alter the anticipated out come?

For all its promise, despite its apparent benefits, our science and technology are limited because we are limited. Our vision is incomplete. We need only look at the side effects and complications that arise as we attempt to control all the increasing complexities of our efforts. How often do we suffer the results of having outsmarted ourselves?

Science and technology have the ability to be great and useful tools but they are intended to serve us, not the other way around.

Why would we worship something that we have created?

How can we reconcile science and faith?

What if archeologists unearthed Noah's Ark, Eden or the foundations of Babel tomorrow? What if science demonstrated beyond a doubt the existence of the elusive "God Particle"? Would it change the heart of a true believer in either science or religion? Arguments would erupt, plausible sounding explanations would abound and at the end of the day would it truly make any difference?

Probably not.

People can and will debate evolution, fossil records and religious relics from now until doom cracks. To what point? Does God's divinity depend on his ability to part the waters, walk on them or change them into wine? Do we worship miracles, or God?

The real question should be, if He did not make the lame walk or the blind see would you follow Him anyway?

Technology has done as much as that. Should we worship at the feet of such men of science? The power of God emanates from every rock and tree – it's found in the simple truths of the Sermon on the Mount, in the commandments to love God and love our neighbor.

Faith demands no miracles.

<u>It is the miracle</u>
…and it lies sleeping with each one of us.

What is it about our nature that makes winning so imperative, we must dominate, we must have all the answers? Is it our insecurity because we are imperfect?

The existence of either faith or science should not be dependant upon the elimination or even subjugation of the other one. The word science comes from Latin, it means "to know" but faith is based in belief. So why can't the two simply co-exist? Render unto Caesar that which is Caesar's and unto God that which is God's?

Science attempts to discover how – Faith endeavors to show us why.

What is the purpose of life?

Ultimately, the purpose of life is to become. By that I mean that at the end of days we will lay the sum total of who we are based on the choices we've made at the feet of our Maker.

When we stop and try to see each other as pilgrims on this common journey through life, we may realize our burdens are not as great as we thought and find it in our hearts to be more tolerant, more patient and a little more willing to help a stranger on their chosen path even when we do not agree with it.

You cannot truly love someone unless you respect them first, even to the point of respecting their right to be wrong. The bible tells us that Moses and his people wandered for forty years, but it doesn't say they were lost. Wandering is a natural part of becoming. We all make mistakes, the trick is to learn from them, to pick ourselves up and try to do better. Be patient and hope that others can be patient with you.

Technology has conspired to rob us of patience. We live in an age of instant everything. Waiting is equated with losing. As a result deferred gratification has gone the way of the Tyrannosaur.

But God and faith work on their own schedule. Life itself is in a sense our baptism and our confirmation may be found in our last breath.

To become takes a lifetime, get comfortable with the idea.

What is the purpose of death?

If there is life after death anyway, what is the purpose of death?

In each of us there is a divine spark, a soul that resides, trapped here. It is like a child that has been entrusted to us. Each of us is its foster parent on earth. It is ours to nurture and like a child we choose how to raise it. We expose it to what is good and bad, what is healthy and unhealthy.

Like a parent of a small child, we choose where it lives, where it goes to school, who its friends are. We pick out its books and clothes and television shows. We take it church and to visit grandparents.

We teach it to venerate age and wisdom, to seek truth and justice, to play fair, to respect others, to develop a sense of honor, to value love, work and sacrifice…

…or not.

Death is when we bid our soul goodbye and send it home to its Father, to see how we did.

What about love, the word is so over used?

St Paul said, "...faith, hope and charity and the greatest of these, is charity." Charity is unconditional love, because it is love without any expectation of return or reward. In the process of becoming that which we might be, what higher sense can we aspire to? All too often we put a price tag on our love and in the process, cheapen it.

That is because we are dealing in the wrong currency. You can only purchase love with love, faithfulness with faith, respect with respect. Such qualities cannot be bought and sold. They are gifts to be treasured and passed on.

It is easy to see why people become jaded. We live in an age when the meaning of love has become skewed and distorted. We can love our cars and our favorite sports teams even though they cannot love us back. Yet marriages have become disposable, our children and elderly are cast aside for the sake of convenience. How ironic.

The nuclear and extended family was the cornerstone of human civilization for tens of thousands of years. Love and respect were the mortar that held it together. Is it any wonder we are a society in peril.

It is a simple matter to find fault with those we love. You need only look; after all we are flawed creatures. But you do not love a person because they are perfect, you love them in spite of the fact that they are not. That is why we act most like God when we can find it in our hearts to forgive.

Over forty years ago my old pastor defined love this way. He said love was giving a person what they need but what we need is often not what we want and what we want is usually not what we need. If we love God we must give Him what He needs. We must make the right choices even when no one is looking. We must love one another even when we are not very loveable.

You bind yourself to that which you love. What are you bound to and can it love you back?

Faith and religion, aren't they the same thing?

The two terms will often be used interchangeably but God made the gift of faith, already ageless when Earth was new. Man made religion in its image. Much the same way that the bible may hold the word of God but the work is written in the words of men.

Faith is built upon questions, which can only be answered in our own hearts.

Religion is built upon doctrine, which is about providing general answers. As such it gives us a sense of direction, form, familiarity, comfort, community and more... but we must still each find faith on our own or it is form without substance, it is direction that lacks purpose.

Religion is about a community but faith is personal. Religion is static; it must be because it is a rock, a foundation on which to build but faith is dynamic, vibrant and alive. Faith must grow stronger and deeper or it languishes. That is why the process of questioning is so imperative to faith.

It is the challenge of searching for those answers that makes us stronger over time. Questions shake our beliefs and cause us to reinforce them or correct our course where needed.

Faith doesn't fear questions, it needs them.

What if I had a bad experience with the church?

Was it with the church, or was it with a member of its clergy?

Perhaps it was with some overly zealous, misguided or hypocritical practitioner(s)?

We have all met people speaking and acting as though they might have or be some authority, yet behaving in ways that would hardly be considered very Godly or Christian.

Remember, they are only people too. They are subject to the same faults and failings as the rest of us. We have to learn to separate the individual from the institution (and it is not always easy).

Consider there might be some value in what such people are trying to say but it may get lost in the personalities. If you can, sift through it rather than discarding what they say outright. Try to weigh the message against their motives and methods. You may discover something lurking there you can find benefit in. If nothing else consider it a lesson in patience. God does ask us to practice forgiveness after all.

However if we surrender control over that aspect of our lives to another person, we risk letting them take God away from us. Adversity should only serve to strengthen our resolve.

If someone blocks the path, find a way around but don't give up.

How can I forgive others who have hurt me?

The act of forgiveness is really about healing your own heart. It is a gift that you give yourself.

Enemies and strangers don't care about you. If they did, they wouldn't be your enemies or strangers. If you harbor anger and resentment toward them, it does them no harm but it does poison you. It drags you down. It takes the hurt they have leveled against you and recycles it over and over. You may not have had control over the situation when they injured you, but by internalizing it you are giving them your permission to go right on hurting you. It is only the act of forgiveness that stops that cycle of pain and puts you beyond their reach. Only you can do this, so why wouldn't you?

When family or friends hurt you, stop and ask yourself why? If it was inadvertent, wouldn't they feel as badly as you, they may not even realize it happened – why permit something like that to fester when you have the power to heal it for both you and them? If you believe that their action was intentional, they meant to hurt you, ask them why? If these are people who love you, why would they purposely hurt you? Something terrible must gnaw at them to cause them to lash out against others they care about. Maybe it was something you said or did unknowingly. Maybe you were merely "convenient" the brunt of anger they can't deal with. Either way, as much as you need the gift of forgiveness, they may need it even more to heal their soul. Why would you withhold that from someone you love?

There are also people who are so filled with anger, rage and violence that they represent a danger to themselves and others. They need help but don't allow your forgiving heart to place you in harm's pathway. Forgiving is not forgetting and love requires that we give a person what they need, even though they may not want it.

There is one last person that desperately needs your forgiveness, you. Sometimes that is the hardest thing in the world to do, because it often requires that we go and beg the forgiveness of those we have hurt. That means facing not only what we have done or failed to do but also the ones we injured in the process.

Yet how else can we every truly lay our burden aside? If we cannot do that, how can we help unburden others? Life is an uphill struggle and some of the heaviest things that weigh down on our heart are anger and resentment. Why would we wish to carry them one second longer than we have to?

We are imperfect but that should not be an excuse for failing. It should serve as an inspiration, a hurdle for us to over come. When we fall, it is forgiveness that picks us up and dusts us off... but it comes with a price. We must actively seek forgiveness from others and from God. We must make amends, learn from those mistakes and try not to repeat them. It is our obligation to be all the more tolerant of others when they stumble, because we know what it is like. Part of the price of forgiveness, is forgiving others.

Consider the example of Christ who committed no wrong yet suffered torture and death but found it within his heart to forgive those who did this to Him and ask yourself, what wrong have I suffered in my life that is so unforgivable?

Then ask, why carry such a burden, when you could lay it down?

What about the end of the world?

A very short parable; three men left for work one morning. One did not own an umbrella and thought such things were just a nuisance. One had an umbrella but left it at home. The third carried his umbrella even though it was only cloudy. It poured. Two men got soaked, one stayed dry.

Mankind will be extinguished someday and the world as we know it will be obliterated. Science and religion both agree on that point. Does it really matter exactly how it will happen? No one will be around to say, "I told you so." No one knows when this will occur, although man as for centuries tried to deduce that exact fatal moment. The Mayan calendar, the pyramid inch, the book of Revelations... why? So that we can outsmart the process, is that the answer? Christ repeatedly said you won't know when the end is coming. Just be ready... like our friend above with his umbrella at hand.

I am mortal. This body needs food, water and rest. I will die some day. There is nothing in this world that is going to change that. Do I need to know where and when I will close my eyes for the last time? No, I don't, it doesn't matter.

None of us can cheat death but we can choose how to live life.

Everything is here for a reason, even you and I. The world is filled with beautiful and joyful things. It is also filled with terrible and hateful things. In the midst of it all we get to choose. Strangely, some people elect to pursue the latter.

Some live their lives only for themselves. Their universe extends no further than their fingertips. They are absorbed with their own imagined self-importance. Yet the mightiest kings and potentates in history have all eventually gone to dust, food for worms. Having lived their lives focused exclusively on their desires, lives that isolated and insulated them from everyone and everything around them, lives consumed with "wanting more". Don't you think they would perish feeling unfulfilled? After all there is always something left to do, something else to acquire, to conquer. For such a person death steals away all that matters to them. I have heard it said that's why they don't put pockets in shrouds.

People discuss and debate immortality. Put aside the realm of sacred belief for a moment and consider the following. All that is tangible passes away, only the intangible continues. It is not about what we have but what we give. How we conduct ourselves in our brief stay upon this planet places its immortal mark on the legacy we leave behind us. In the course of our lives if we are cruel, thoughtless, self-centered and grasping don't we propagate that in the others around us? In the same token if we are honest, industrious, considerate, helpful, kind and loving people don't we become examples that inspire the best qualities in the lives we touch? In the annals of history, if you are "lucky" you may serve as a dusty footnote. However the good and bad we do are recycled throughout the ages in how our great grandchildren's children will think and act. Our names may be lost through the years but the pain of a critical word and the power of a smile endure.

Christ never traveled more than a few miles from where He was born but He preached a message of hope, love and forgiveness to the small handful that could hear His words. Two thousand years later His name and His teachings are still revered around the world but to my knowledge nobody recalls the person who first invented crucifixion.

The world will end. That is a given. How and when that will happen really doesn't matter. God will take care of that.

It isn't about when or how the world will die, it is about when and how will you live?

Why was Judas "the consummate secular man"?

He walked with Christ, ate with Him, listened to Him – yet he rejected and betrayed Him for what…some paltry worldly sum. Isn't that what we do every day when we ask God to take a backseat to our worldly concerns?

Judas was Adam's counterpart in the New Testament. He played a critical part in the fulfillment of God's Will. In fact it demonstrates that <u>the existence of the secular mind is absolutely essential to belief</u> because it is adversarial.

Without doubt, there is no certainty.
Without weakness, there is no strength.
Without fear, there is no valor.
Without greed there, is no charity.

True faith does not compete with our secular existence. It is found in our ability to accept God as integral to our growth and well-being in the midst of all this. It does not change our existence, but it does change how we see and react to it.

It is about choice.

But what if I am a bad person?

For whatever reason, there are people who have given themselves over to evil, but that is usually not the case.

Good people can do bad things and even bad people can do good things. The fact that you recognize you may have made some poor choices in your life means that you possess a sense of right and wrong.

That's a pretty good start.

There is always a road back. It begins by recognizing our faults, making amends, learning from our errors and trying to do better. Believe me, you are not alone. We all make mistakes. It helps keep the band aid manufacturers in business.

I think that the most compelling aspect of Christianity is that God recognizes our imperfections and challenges because He chose to live as one of us. God knows what it means as a human to be tempted. Think about the power of that statement. When He forgives us it is not just from some lofty perch. He knows all the heartache and all the pain that we face on a daily basis. When He asks us to forgive one another and love one another, He knows how hard and how rewarding that can be too.

It helps to remember that even the best of us will never be perfect in the course of our lives. That should never stop us from trying to better our selves, it should goad us on. Seek help from God and those around you. When we think and act as a community, when we believe that we are all connected, when one of us gets better – don't we all get better?

There will always be lots of dead ends and bad turns. You can expect that but don't let setbacks become an excuse to fail. You are better than that.

Mistakes are like rocks in the path. Some are pebbles that we trip over. Some are boulders that block our way. When we carry them with us, they weigh us down. When we learn from them and leave them behind they can become stepping stones for all those who follow after.

The time to start climbing is before we sink any deeper. Grab hold.

Afterward:

I have tried to keep this work as small and brief as possible so that it would read quickly and be easy to carry - after all it's a long road. Toward that end I should be thankful (and so should you) for my limited wit and wisdom or I might be tempted to prattle on indefinitely.

The purpose of this book is to present an argument for the necessity for faith to a secular world. Regardless of where you are on your journey, I hope this helps you in some small way on your path and that it encourages you to share with others just as I am sharing with you.

It is written from a Christian perspective but I believe much of it has application in other religions.

God bless and God speed.

About the author:

Paul Holland had the uncommon wisdom to marry his best friend over thirty years ago and together they managed to raise three fine young people.

The rest, is incidental.

www.ingramcontent.com/pod-product-compliance
Lightning Source LLC
Chambersburg PA
CBHW071311060426
42444CB00034B/1937